This book belongs to:

Name

Address

Other details